ON THE SCENE

A CSI's Life

Diana Herweck

CRIME SCENE

CRIME SCENE - DO NOT

E SCENE - DO NOT

Consultants

Timothy Rasinski, Ph.D.
Kent State University

Lori Oczkus
Literacy Consultant

Dani Mata
Forensic Scientist

Based on writing from
TIME For Kids. *TIME For Kids* and the *TIME For Kids* logo are registered trademarks of TIME Inc. Used under license.

Publishing Credits

Dona Herweck Rice, *Editor-in-Chief*
Lee Aucoin, *Creative Director*
Jamey Acosta, *Senior Editor*
Heidi Fiedler, *Editor*
Lexa Hoang, *Designer*
Stephanie Reid, *Photo Editor*
Rane Anderson, *Contributing Author*
Rachelle Cracchiolo, *M.S.Ed., Publisher*

Image Credits: p.5 (bottom left), 35 Alamy; cover & pp.1, 4, 6 (bottom),17, 24 (bottom), p.30 Getty Images; pp.14, 18, 22, 24, 24 (top), p.34 iStockphoto; p.41 LOC_A. Weidenbach; p.10 Photo Reseachers Inc.; pp.21, 25, 28–29, 32–33 Timothy J. Bradley; p.37 Zaid Hamid [Public Domain] via. Wikimedia; p.31 AFP/Newscom; p.26 EPA/Newscom; p.20 (bottom) ZUMA Press/Newscom; All other images from Shutterstock.

Teacher Created Materials

5301 Oceanus Drive
Huntington Beach, CA 92649-1030
http://www.tcmpub.com
ISBN 978-1-4333-4825-9
© 2013 Teacher Created Materials, Inc.

Table of Contents

On the Scene

The house is covered in blood. A body is floating out back in the swimming pool. Was it an accident or **foul play**? When did this happen? And who is responsible? Where should investigators start?

Those are the questions crime scene investigators (CSIs) must answer. CSIs study crime scenes. They collect **evidence** to find out what happened. It's just like on a TV show, but this is real. And the science they use to do their jobs is a matter of life and death.

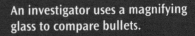

An investigator uses a magnifying glass to compare bullets.

THINK LINK

Imagine you are a CSI.
➤ What skills would you need to succeed?
➤ How would you solve a crime?
➤ Why do you think this job is so important?

3

DO NOT CROSS

DO NOT

CRIME SCEN

DO NOT

CRIME SCENE
INVESTIGATOR

LAS VEGAS

C.S.I.

NEVADA

POLICE

5

Traces of Evidence

When someone commits a crime—however big or small—there are traces of evidence. Even a simple crime, such as stealing a cookie, leaves clues behind. Most criminals try to avoid leaving signs of their work. But evidence can be so small it's nearly invisible. The average person won't see it, but a CSI knows exactly where to look.

CSIs look for many types of evidence. Basic marks like fingerprints, mud, lipstick, and ink can give clues about the crime. **Fibers** from plants, hair, clothes, and furniture can be traced to the scene of the crime, too. CSIs even search for patterns in mud. One footprint can lead them to the **perpetrator** (PUR-pi-trey-ter).

CIVILIAN CRIME FIGHTERS

Most CSIs are **civilians**. This means they might not carry guns. They don't arrest people or give tickets. They help police officers and detectives solve crimes. But they are not police officers.

Photographs provide a permanent record of a crime scene and the evidence.

EVIDENCE

13

7

DIG DEEPER!

Extreme Experts

There are many ways to solve a crime. That's why CSI teams are made up of many specialists. Depending on the crime, different specialists will be called in to help.

Latent print examiners (LEYT-nt PRINT ig-ZAM-in-ers) specialize in fingerprints.

Some scientists specialize in finding **DNA** matches.

Odontologists (oh-don-TOL-uh-justs) can identify a body by its teeth. This can be helpful if there is damage to the other parts of the body.

Pathologists (puh-THOL-uh-justs) study the human body. They can determine the cause of death, the time of death, and more.

Entomologists (en-tuh-MOL-uh-justs) study insects and their behavior. Insects help determine the area where something took place as well as when it happened.

Some CSIs are **ballistics** (buh-LIS-tiks) experts. They study guns and bullets.

Forensic (fuh-REN-sik) **photographers** take pictures of evidence.

Forensic artists listen to **witnesses** and review evidence. They use clues to draw a picture of the people who commit crimes so police officers can look for them.

Looking for Tracks

The investigation starts outside. CSIs begin by looking for tracks. These clues can lead to the **suspect**. Shoe prints in the dirt might show what kind of shoe the suspect wore. If it's a special kind of shoe, the CSI may be able to learn where the shoe was sold. The CSI might even be able to look at receipts from the store. This could reveal who bought the shoes.

Or there might be tire tracks. Studying the tracks narrows down which kind of car was there. Detectives can find out if anyone saw that kind of car during the crime.

A CSI will search the crime scene for fibers. Perhaps the suspect's clothes tore on something. Maybe a hair fell on the ground.

A CSI looks for evidence that shows where the car has been.

TRACKING TOGETHER

Computer programs collect information from labs across the country. One program focuses on the tracks left behind by tires. The program compares tire marks to the over 5,000 tracks stored. This helps CSIs catch criminals who are on the move.

large truck tracks

automobile tracks

bicycle tracks

truck tracks

Make It Count

After a crime, every second counts. Investigators need to be ready to work day or night. Below is a sample of what a CSI might do during regular work hours. But a CSI could be collecting evidence in the middle of the night and be back at the lab before the sun comes up!

6:00 A.M.   Wake up, get dressed, and eat breakfast.

7:30 A.M.   Arrive at the lab and review yesterday's work.

8:00 A.M.   A call comes in. You are needed at a crime scene.

8:30 A.M.   Arrive at the scene of the crime and talk with the team.

10:00 A.M.   Look for evidence. Collect samples of anything to be reviewed at the lab.

11:00 A.M.   Find and lift fingerprints. Take photographs of the scene.

1:00 P.M.   Return to the lab with evidence. Meet with the team to discuss the crime.

1:30 P.M   Search the **database** for matching prints.

3:00 P.M   Send evidence out for DNA analysis.

3:30 P.M.   Meet with the team to exchange information. Begin writing your report.

6:00 P.M   Wrap up and head home for the day.

Assess, Look, Analyze

CSIs follow three basic steps to learn about a crime.

ASSESS

First, they **assess** the scene. When CSIs arrive at the crime scene, they rope off the area. They must protect the area and keep people out. This prevents **tampering** with the evidence. Other detectives tell the CSI their theories about what happened.

LOOK

Next, they look for evidence. The hunt for evidence begins. The CSIs walk back and forth in a **grid**. Walking in this pattern helps them cover every inch. Evidence is carefully stored in bags and other containers.

ANALYZE

Finally, they **analyze** the evidence. The CSIs return to the lab to analyze the evidence. They study bullets. They compare drugs and explosives. Computers make sound or video clips clearer. They also run DNA tests on blood samples and hair. After all the tests, they'll write a report and present their findings.

Finding Fingerprints

At the crime scene, CSIs look for fingerprints. A set of prints can be a valuable clue. The CSI often searches the crime-scene entrance for fingerprints. A burglar may have left fingerprints on a window or a weapon. The CSI will ask witnesses if any objects have been moved. Broken lamps, drawers, and light switches are smart places to look for prints. The CSI may fingerprint people who live in the house. These prints can be compared to others found in the house. The CSI must learn which prints don't belong.

Computers compare prints from suspects around the world.

NATURAL INK

Oils fill the **ridges** on our fingers. When our fingers touch something, the oils leave a print. Even when the oil dries, the image remains. A trained CSI can "dust" the fingerprint to make it more visible.

FIND IT FAST

Every print is compared to the prints stored in a database. On TV, a computer quickly matches the prints. In real life, it may take over an hour to match a fingerprint. It takes time, but it works.

Each ridge in the fingerprint is another point to compare.

DNA Discoveries

In the 1980s, scientists found a new way to analyze evidence. CSIs can now use DNA to solve crimes. DNA is in every living thing. DNA is in saliva. It's in urine. And it's in blood. DNA can be found in a strand of hair. It can even be found in tears. Just like a fingerprint, everyone's DNA is unique. And like fingerprints, people leave DNA behind without even knowing it. DNA can be found on a cigarette. There might be DNA on a cup the suspect used. CSIs **swab** many types of evidence to look for DNA.

A DNA molecule is made up of two long microscopic strands that twist around each other like a spiral staircase.

COLD CASES

Some cases have never been solved. It's usually because there isn't enough evidence to convict a criminal. These types of cases are called *cold cases*. DNA evidence has helped CSIs solve cold cases more than 20 years after a crime was committed!

When an investigation is going well, detectives say they are hot on the trail of the suspect. But when they are unable to find new evidence or learn more, they say the trail has run cold.

Investigators use a clean cotton swab to collect samples of DNA. The samples are stored in tubes to protect the evidence.

Paper Trail

Not all evidence involves blood or fingerprints. Many crimes are solved by looking at the papers criminals leave behind. **Document analysts** look for clues on paper. Receipts, e-mails, and calendars can all be used as evidence. Document analysts study handwriting, too. This helps them learn clues about the suspect. Other CSIs are experts on analyzing different inks and papers. What a person writes on paper can be used in court. Many cases involving **fraud** depend on paper trails to convict the criminal.

CSIs dust a special powder onto a document. Used correctly, it can reveal where a rubber eraser was used.

IN WRITING

A plain piece of paper may look boring, but it may be the key to finding the truth. These documents can all lead investigators to the truth.

contracts   **receipts**   **emails**

date books   **love letters**

Bullet Basics

Sometimes, the police find bullet **casings** at the scene. These are often used as evidence. The casing can tell a CSI what type of bullet was used. CSIs can also learn about the model of the gun. This can lead police to the shop where the gun was purchased. Once this is known, they may be able to find out who bought the gun.

BALLISTICS

Ballistics is the science of what happens when a gun is fired. Ballistics experts can tell what happened when the bullet left the gun. They can determine where the bullet landed. They can even tell how close the **victim** was to the gun.

BOUNCING BALL

A bullet can travel a great distance in a short space. Bullets move at such fast speeds that they can travel through walls or anything else in their path. Study the diagram below to see where these bullets traveled.

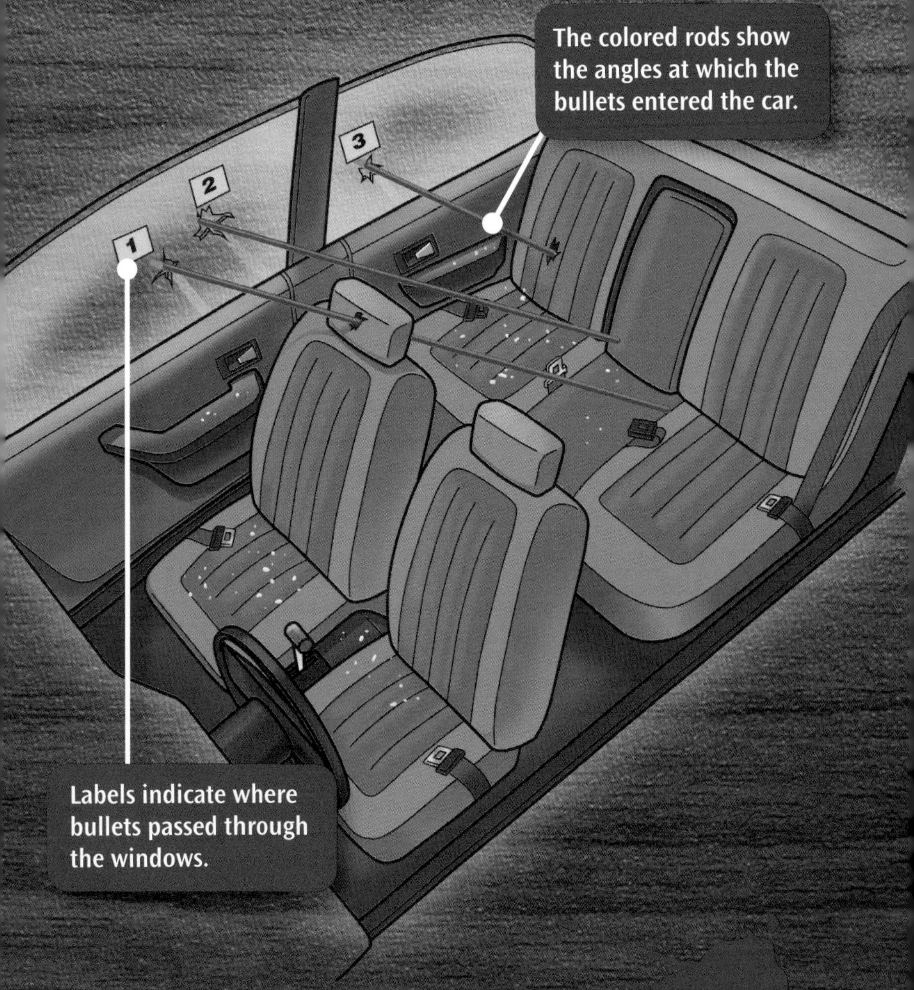

The colored rods show the angles at which the bullets entered the car.

Labels indicate where bullets passed through the windows.

Clues That Crawl

Insects are often the first to arrive at the scene of a crime. Forensic entomologists arrive soon after. They quickly collect insects from the victim's body. CSIs study the size of the insects. This helps them know how much time has passed since the crime took place. Insects are attracted to wet areas in the body. Flies often lay eggs in the eyes or mouth. If bugs are found around a specific body part, it may mean that area was bleeding or injured. Flies can find a dead body within minutes of death. They have been known to fly over a mile to reach a body.

BUG BASICS

Every detail at a crime scene is important—even a creepy-crawly one. Entomologists follow these steps when they collect evidence.

1. Take samples of insects and blood from around the body.

2. Note the type of crime scene. Is it indoors or outdoors? Is it in a dry desert or a humid forest?

3. Look for evidence of other animals. Are birds feeding on the insects? Birds often wait until insects appear. If other species are at the scene, it may mean the body has been there a while.

4. Check the temperature of the area. Is it hot or cold? Is there a fan on, or are there large areas of shade?

5. Compare the insects to samples in the lab. If eggs have hatched and young insects are found, the body has most likely been dead longer.

6. Revisit the crime scene to confirm the temperature of the area. Insects grow faster in high temperatures. The colder it is, the slower they will develop. Or if it is very cold, insects might not be found at all. But that doesn't mean the body hasn't been there for weeks.

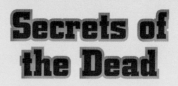

DIG DEEPER!

Secrets of the Dead

A forensic pathologist studies a **corpse** to learn the cause of death. It is the pathologist's job to find out if a person died because of an illness or an accident. Or perhaps the victim was harmed by someone else. These CSIs look for clues in every organ of the body. When pathologists study a mysterious death, they have to answer many questions. What happened? Who committed the crime? What weapon was used? When did it happen?

Pathologists study the land and weather. Knowing if it rained recently or if the air is dry helps CSIs calculate the time of death.

DAYS OF DECAY

Finding out when a crime was committed is important. Forensic pathologists study the victim's body and compare it to this time line.

3–6 hours

Fresh Stage

The skin turns blue and purple. The muscles in the body become stiff.

1–10 days

Bloat Stage

Gases inside the body build up. Maggots start to feed on the body. Strong odors are present.

10–20 days

Active Decay

Insects feed on the body. Fluids like water, blood, and urine have been lost. The body is losing mass.

20–50 days

Advanced Decay

Little of the body is left. There is less insect activity.

50–365 days

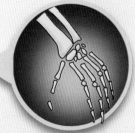

Dry Remains

All that is left of the body is dry skin, bones, and hair.

The Power of Evidence

A CSI's job doesn't end after the investigation. A CSI will often need to appear in court. The CSI will **testify**. It's the CSI's job to explain what the evidence means. The CSI will answer many questions. Nobody wants to make a mistake. The evidence will send a **guilty** person to jail or let an **innocent** person go free. That is why it's so important that CSIs collect evidence carefully. They don't want to miss a clue that could send a criminal to jail.

A ballistics expert notes the size of the gun.

LOOK SHARP

CSIs need to be detail oriented. That means they need to notice the small things. Are you thinking about becoming a CSI? Test yourself! Look at the pictures below and see if you can find at least five differences.

Answers: clock, shoes, magazines, red cylinder near the window, art on the wall, curtain stripe pattern, file drawer rotated 45°, height of blinds, bookcase shelves transposed

27

In the Lab

CSIs do much of their work away from the crime scene. The lab is where CSIs analyze the evidence. This is where investigators can learn if there is a match to fingerprints or tire tracks. Evidence can be linked to possible suspects and other crimes. All evidence is **catalogued** so it's easy to find and keep safe. The lab is also where CSIs meet to discuss their work and write their reports.

analyzing fibers with a powerful microscope

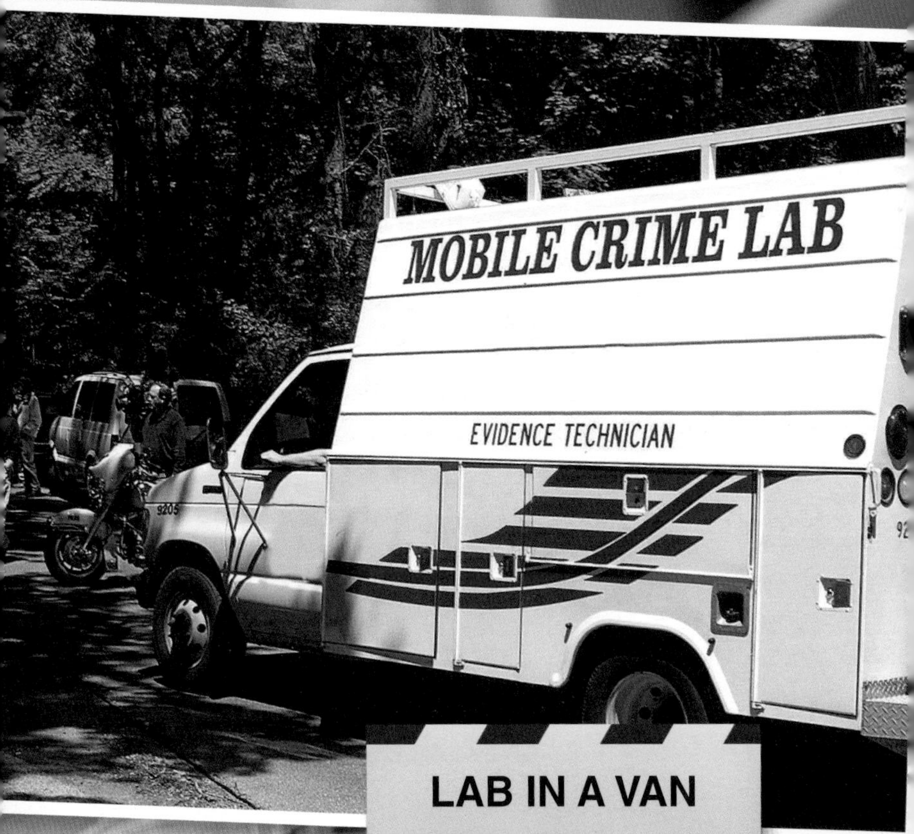

MOBILE CRIME LAB

EVIDENCE TECHNICIAN

9205

92

LAB IN A VAN

CSIs travel between the crime scene and the lab in special vans. Each van has all the tools needed for collecting evidence at the scene, including electricity and phones. This lets investigators stay at the scene for several days at a time.

Each year, the nation's crime labs handle over one million cases.

DIG DEEPER!

Tools of the Trade

CSIs use many tools to help them better understand the evidence found in the field. New products come out every year. The most common tools are shown here. Check them out!

CSIs do not wear police uniforms. But they need to dress comfortably.

Swab boxes hold liquid samples.

Tweezers, scissors, and pliers are used to collect evidence.

Plastic tubes hold sand, dirt, fibers, and powder taken from the crime scene.

Brushes and tape are used to collect fingerprints.

Scalpels cut pieces of evidence.

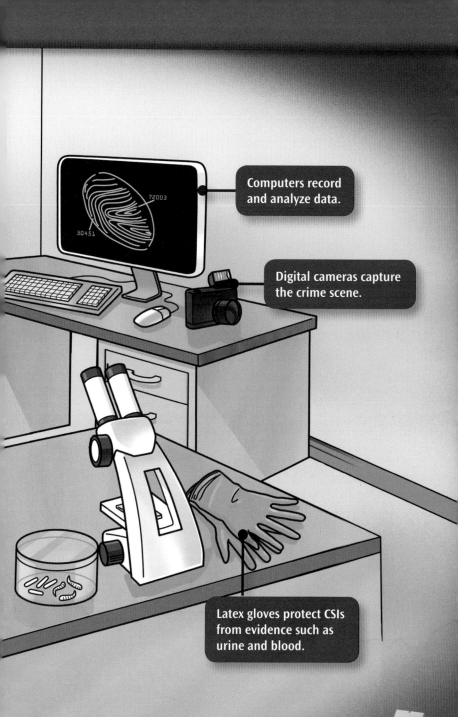

Computers record and analyze data.

Digital cameras capture the crime scene.

Latex gloves protect CSIs from evidence such as urine and blood.

Writing a Report

After the CSI analyzes the evidence, it's time to write a report. It must be very detailed. The report includes all the actions taken at the scene of the crime. It notes the analysis performed in the lab. Photographs, sketches, and test results are all included. The report will be reviewed by another CSI for accuracy. Police officers will use the report to finish their investigation and arrest suspects. The report may be used when the case goes to **trial**.

CSIs need to take good notes as they work. They often number the pages of their notebooks. A pen is used to avoid smudges. If they make a mistake, CSIs draw a line through it and write their initials next to it. They never skip pages or destroy notes.

34

MAKE A NOTE

CSIs must write neatly. Their notes are reviewed by other CSIs, detectives, and lawyers. There may be information that doesn't seem important at the time. But it could make sense hours or days later.

Case Number: 543027391	Date: 9/30/13
Event Occurred Between: 9/30/13 at 5:30 and 9/30/13 at 5:45 A.M.	
Time Arrived on the Scene: 6:05 A.M.	
Offense: Burglary	
Location: 5492 Hollingswood Drive, Vanite, KY, 48309	
Victims: 1	**Vehicles Stolen:** 1
Forced Entry: Yes	**Weapon Type:** Unknown
Reporting Officer: H. Spade	**ID#:** 00483

Report Summary:

On September 30, 2013, I was sent to 5492 Hollingswood Drive. I was responding to a stolen vehicle complaint. The initial responding officer briefed the CSI team. We secured the driveway, garage, and house. Skid marks in the street were immediately observed. A large puddle marked the driveway.

Case Closed

What does it take to become a crime scene investigator? CSIs are committed to learning the truth. They are curious about the past. And they are passionate about **justice**. The best CSIs love working with people and learning new things. Every CSI needs a strong scientific background.

CSIs also need a college **degree**. The degree should be in one of the sciences. Many CSIs have a degree in biology, chemistry, or physics. Some departments look for a person with a degree in forensic science. CSIs need at least two years of training in their specialty. During training, CSIs spend time in the classroom. They also spend time in the lab. And they **shadow** CSIs in the field. They must pass many tests to prove they understand how to perform the job.

Some high schools offer classes in forensics. Some summer programs offer classes for even younger kids. It's never too early to get started training as a CSI!

Police perform background checks to be sure the CSI team is trustworthy and reliable.

FOOTPRINTS

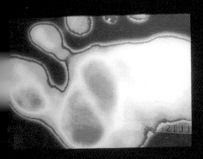

DID YOU KNOW?

ough fingerprints receive the attention, footprint evidence been admitted in U.S. courts 1934.

like your fingerprints, there are ct patterns on the soles and of your feet, which are pletely unique to you.

"footprints" don't get a lot of ci, the military keeps inked essions of the bare feet of flight nnel on file since feet are better cted and preserved than hands e event of a crash or fire.

SHOE PRINTS

Since few people walk around barefoot, a database of shoeprints seemed like a smart idea. So smart, in fact, that one company created The Bonaparte Image Capture and Retrieval (BICAR), a vital tool in the pursuit of criminals.

The BICAR system relies on footwear manufacturers providing samples of their sole designs for inclusion in the "Solemate" database, which includes thousands upon thousands of tread samples from shoes around the world.

WATCH YOUR STEP

The Crime Museum in Washington, DC, teaches visitors about police work and crime scene investigations. You can gather clues needed for the investigation, explore a CSI lab, learn about safety, and more.

Scientific Sleuths

When a crime occurs, it can change lives forever. The most dangerous crimes make us afraid. But with every crime, there is evidence. And with evidence, there can be justice. Crime scene investigators use science to uncover the truth. They find the clues that others miss. From a plain receipt to a puddle of blood, CSIs study the scene to solve every kind of crime. The work they do requires a brave heart and a passion for science. Above all, they must be willing to follow the truth until it leads to justice.

"The administration of justice is the firmest pillar of good government."

— George Washington

Dani Mata is a forensic scientist in California. She specializes in drug analysis. When asked about her favorite part of the job, she quickly answered, "Helping people!" Find out more about her work below.

How did you become a CSI?

I have a bachelor's degree in chemistry and a master's of science in forensic science. I interned for the Illinois State Police Department. When I was a kid, I really wanted to be a police officer. I learned in middle school that I did not want to pass out traffic tickets but loved math and science. So I figured the best way to be in law enforcement and apply my love for math and science was to study forensics. In high school and college, I took every class that would help me get a job in forensics.

What's a typical day like for you?

In the morning, I pull samples to test for drugs. These samples can include blood, urine, brain, liver, and stomach contents. The brain, liver, and stomach contents must be blended and diluted with water before testing. While those samples are being analyzed, I write up reports for samples that are done. I may also have to go to court to testify on a completed case.

In what ways is your job different from the CSI work shown on TV?

I only work in the lab and only in one section. On TV, one person often does many different jobs. At most labs, it is not like that. You are trained to be an expert in one or two areas. It takes many people, including CSIs, police officers, and lawyers, to solve a crime.

Glossary

analyze—to study and think about

assess—to find out the size and type of something, often a problem

ballistics—the science that studies guns and the motions of bullets

casings—the coverings on bullets

catalogued—entered into a list in a systematic way

civilians—people who are not in military, law enforcement, or firefighting organizations

corpse—a dead body

database—a complete collection of related data, generally in a computer

degree—a certificate received after completing college

DNA—the chemical that makes up all living things; it carries genetic information; each person has a unique DNA

document analysts—people who search for clues on paper

entomologists—scientists who study insects and their behavior

evidence—facts that help people make conclusions

fibers—fine threadlike pieces of fabric or plants

forensic artists—people who draw or sculpt to assist in an investigation

forensic photographers—people who take photographs of evidence to assist in an investigation

foul play—dishonest behavior that causes harm, often violent

fraud—something that is dishonest and deceitful

grid—a pattern of horizontal and perpendicular lines

guilty—having done something wrong

innocent—free from legal wrong

justice—rightfulness or lawfulness

latent print examiners—people who specialize in analyzing fingerprints

odontologists—scientists who study teeth and their surrounding tissues

pathologists—scientists who study the human body and diseases

perpetrator—a person who committed a crime

ridges—narrow raised strips

scalpels—small, straight knives used to cut cloth or skin

shadow—to follow and watch

suspect—someone who is thought to have committed a crime

swab—to use a bit of cotton on a stick to collect samples, such as saliva

tampering—altering, damaging, or misusing evidence to change an outcome

testify—to give evidence in court

trial—an examination before a judge

victim—a person who has been hurt or affected by a crime

witnesses—people who see or hear crimes

Index

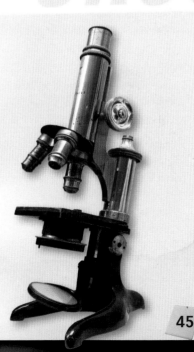

Bibliography

Prokos, Anna. *Guilty by a Hair! Real-Life DNA Matches!* **Franklin Watts, 2007.**

This book examines the importance of DNA in investigations, in both convicting and freeing people. It explains where DNA can be found on a person and where it can be left behind at a crime scene.

Schulz, Karen K. *CSI Expert: Forensic Science for Kids.* **Prufrock Press, 2008.**

This book includes more than 25 in-depth activities on fingerprinting, evidence collection, blood-stain identification, forensic careers, and much more.

Standards-Based Investigations: Forensic Science. **Shell Education, 2008.**

Over 30 activities teach you to observe, organize and record data, think critically, and conduct simple tests to solve crimes ranging from blood samples to handwriting.

Webber, Diane. *Shot and Framed: Photographers at the Crime Scene.* **Franklin Watts, 2007.**

You will learn what forensic photographers do and study cases from the past.

Wiese, Jim. *Detective Science: 40 Crime-Solving, Case-Breaking, Crook-Catching Activities for Kids.* **John Wiley, 1996.**

This book shows how detectives and forensic experts use science to do their jobs and presents experiments that explore forensic science and criminal investigation.

More to Explore

PBS Kids

http://pbskids.org/fetch

Ruff, the investigative dog, leads students through an interactive investigation, picking up and analyzing clues after something has been stolen. Click on *Games* at the bottom to see all *Fetch!* games. There are three CSI ones.

CSI: The Experience

http://forensics.rice.edu

Characters from the CBS show *CSI* lead you through the basics of forensic science.

Forensics for Kids

http://www.wartgames.com/themes/science/forensics.html

This website links to a variety of forensic games, activities, and presentations.

Kids Ahead

http://kidsahead.com

Choose *Subjects* at the bottom, then click on *Crime Scene Investigation.* This website lists activities, projects, articles, and events across the country relating to forensics.

Kids Camps

http://www.kidscamps.com

Visit this site to learn more about CSI summer camps. Scroll down and click on *CSI* under *Special Interest Camps.*

About the Author

Diana Herweck has always been interested in the things people do, including their jobs. She works as a teacher and a counselor, helping people of all ages decide what they want to do when they grow up. Just like CSIs, she enjoys helping people. She also loves working with children and spending time with her family. She enjoys playing with her kids, reading, music, movies, and crafts of all sorts, especially scrapbooking. Diana lives in Southern California with her husband, two wonderful children, and three dogs.